Original title:

Wheaten Lullabies Beneath the Unicorn Hue

Author: Lan Donne

ISBN HARDBACK: 978-1-80559-435-2

ISBN PAPERBACK: 978-1-80559-934-0

# The Gentle Murmur of Harvest Winds

Gentle whispers flow through fields,
Caressing grains, nature yields.
Rustling secrets weave the air,
Harvest winds confront despair.

Sunset hues paint the vast sky,
Golden whispers, soft and spry.
Nature's breath, a tender song,
In this haven, we belong.

Beneath the boughs where shadows play,
Time drips slowly, night meets day.
Fleeting moments, life anew,
Breezy notes and skies of blue.

Fields sway gently, a dance divine,
In the twilight, colors shine.
Echoes linger on the breeze,
Harvest winds, our hearts appease.

Stars awaken, the night unfurls,
A lullaby for sleepy worlds.
Together, under moonlight's glow,
In harvest's arms, we feel the flow.

## Fantasies Woven in Wheat Stalks

Wheat stalks sway in rhythmic tune,
Dreams are born beneath the moon.
Golden fields, a tapestry,
Woven tales of mystery.

In the silence, stories grow,
Echoes of the winds that blow.
Nature's brush paints visions bright,
Whispers catch the fading light.

Children laugh as shadows dance,
In this world, we take our chance.
Fantasies drift on the breeze,
Life's adventures, sweet decrees.

Glimmers spark in waving grains,
Stories cradle in their veins.
Starlit canvas, vast and wide,
In this moment, we confide.

Together we'll chase dreams anew,
Through golden fields, me and you.
Wheat stalks whisper, winds dip low,
In their embrace, our spirits flow.

# Ethereal Glow of Mythic Twilight

Ethereal glow paints the land,
Mythic whispers, soft and grand.
The twilight dances on the crest,
Hearts entwined, we find our rest.

Colors blend in a graceful swirl,
As the stars begin to pearl.
Veils of dusk envelop tight,
In this magic, pure delight.

Immortal tales in every sigh,
Underneath the twilight sky.
Legends woven through the night,
In this realm, our souls take flight.

Phantom dreams that gently weave,
In twilight's arms, we dare believe.
Every shadow tells a story,
In the dusk, we seek the glory.

Together under starlit seas,
Bound by dreams and ancient trees.
In the glow, we find our way,
Ethereal light, forever stay.

# Serenading Shadows in Golden Grain

Shadows serenade the dawn,
In golden fields, we are drawn.
Rustling echoes fill the air,
Nature's grace, beyond compare.

Silver beams through stalks will peek,
Softly brushing cheeks and cheek.
Waving grains, a gentle sigh,
In their dance, we feel the high.

Harmony of dusk and dawn,
Whispers linger, love is born.
Every ripple, story shared,
In this vastness, we are fared.

With open hearts, we roam the plain,
Finding solace, without pain.
Golden whispers weave a dream,
In the harvest's gentle gleam.

Together, lost but never alone,
In shadows cast, we make our home.
A serenade for hearts that know,
In golden grain, our spirits grow.

# Lullabies of Pastel Horizons

Soft hues brush the dawn,
Whispers in the air,
Gentle dreams are born,
Cradled without care.

Clouds drift like a sigh,
Painting skies in blush,
A canvas stretched so high,
Embracing morning's hush.

Breezes hum a tune,
Chasing shadows long,
Golden rays commune,
Nature's soothing song.

In the quiet light,
Birds begin to sing,
Lullabies take flight,
As day starts to spring.

Each moment unfolds,
With stories new and bright,
In pastel folds,
The heart finds its light.

# Mystical Glow of Enchanted Fields

Moonlit paths of gold,
Sparkle with delight,
Wandering hearts unfold,
Beneath the starry night.

Whispers in the breeze,
Tell of ancient lore,
Dancing through the trees,
Magic waits in store.

Fields of dreams awaken,
Glistening with dew,
Quiet promises taken,
In shadows deep and new.

Mystical and bright,
The glow calls us near,
Guiding through the night,
Casting off all fear.

Lost in this embrace,
Time drifts like a stream,
In this sacred space,
We wander through a dream.

# Whispered Echoes of the Wheat Waves

Rippling golden seas,
Wheat waves dance and sway,
Carried by the breeze,
In the sun's warm play.

Nature's quiet song,
Rustles through the rows,
Where the heart belongs,
And the spirit knows.

Each stalk tall and bold,
Whispers tales of yore,
A tapestry of gold,
Of those who came before.

Underneath the sky,
Dreams take flight and soar,
As we ponder why,
We seek evermore.

In this vast expanse,
Wheat waves gently call,
Inviting us to dance,
With the world, enthralled.

# Twilight's Serenade Amongst the Meadows

As the day departs,
Twilight starts to play,
With soft, tender hearts,
In a radiant display.

Shadows stretch and blend,
In hues of lilac glow,
Night begins to send,
Whispers we all know.

Fireflies flicker bright,
A serenade begins,
Chasing away night,
With soft, soothing spins.

Meadows weave their tales,
In the dusk's warm light,
While the gentle gales,
Kiss the eve goodnight.

In this tranquil hour,
Nature's song takes flight,
Beneath the soft power,
Of stars shining bright.

## Silhouettes of Magic in the Fading Light

Amidst the dusk, shadows blend,
Whispers of twilight start to send.
Figures dance with grace untold,
Mysteries wrapped in marigold.

The horizon glows, a fiery hue,
As stars awaken, one by two.
In the embrace of evening's charm,
Silhouettes cast by nature's arm.

Night unfolds its velvet cloak,
Veils the world with soft-spoken smoke.
Each star a tale, each breeze a sigh,
Magic lingers where shadows lie.

In this hour when day meets night,
Enchantments blend in soft twilight.
With every flicker, hearts ignite,
Silhouettes whisper of lost delight.

Drawn to the edge of dreams unfurled,
Where quiet wonders linger, swirled.
Here in magic's sweet embrace,
Fading light reveals hidden grace.

# The Enchantment of Grain at Sunset

Golden fields in evening's glow,
Where gentle winds of summer blow.
Grains sway softly, wild and free,
Whispering secrets to the sea.

Crimson skies above unite,
With hues that dance, a pure delight.
Each stalk a story, life's refrain,
In the harvest's warmth, joy remains.

As the day begins to wane,
Nature's beauty, soft and plain.
Capturing moments, time's embrace,
The enchantment of this sacred space.

Beneath the arch of twilight's dome,
The world settles, finds its home.
In the grain's whisper, truth we find,
Heartbeats echo, intertwined.

The sun dips low, a final bow,
A canvas painted, sacred vow.
In this stillness, memories spun,
The harvest's joy, a day well won.

# Shimmering Whispers in Coastal Breezes

Waves crash softly on the shore,
Secrets carried, stories of yore.
Salty air and shimmering light,
Invoke the magic of the night.

Breezes dance with playful glee,
Embracing all who wander free.
In the twilight, spirits sing,
A lullaby the oceans bring.

Starlit skies extend their reach,
While moonbeams kiss the grains of beach.
Shells and stones, their tales revealed,\nIn nature's realm,
our hearts are healed.

As tides embrace the edge of land,
And twilight paints with gentle hand.
Whispers linger, soft and sweet,
In every heartbeat, magic's beat.

The night unfolds, a velvet wave,
Yet in the quiet, we seem brave.
With shimmering whispers, dreams arise,
In coastal breezes, under skies.

# A Song of Color in Pastoral Serenity

Canvas of green meets sky so blue,
In pastoral peace, a tranquil view.
Fields alive with blossoms bright,
Nature's palette, pure delight.

Wandering paths where wildflowers grow,
Gentle streams with their crystal flow.
Every hue a note to sing,
In harmony that spring can bring.

Sunset drapes its golden gown,
Painting landscapes, love renown.
Colors merge in soft embrace,
A song of life, a sacred space.

Underneath the vast expanse,
Fields whisper softly, invite a dance.
Nature's symphony, sweet and clear,
In every petal, love draws near.

As twilight deepens, shadows play,
In serenity, we find our way.
Color's song in evening's light,
Wraps the world in pure delight.

# Cornflowers Dancing in Celestial Light


In fields where blue blooms sway and spin,
Their petals whisper secrets to the wind.
Beneath the sun's warm, gentle gaze,
Cornflowers dance in summer's haze.

With every breeze, they twist and twine,
A ballet pure, a sight divine.
Their color bold against the green,
A stroke of art in Nature's scene.

Skyward they reach, in bold delight,
In harmony with the fading light.
Each blossom vibrant, wild and free,
A fleeting glimpse of eternity.

As day yields softly to the night,
They close their petals, dim the light.
Yet in the dark, their spirits soar,
Cornflowers dream of daylight's encore.

In tomorrow's sun, they will ignite,
With joy anew, a pure delight.
Dancing once more, in fields so bright,
Cornflowers bask in celestial light.

## Sunlit Fantasies on Wheat Horizons

Golden waves beneath the sun,
Wheat fields shimmer, dreams begun.
Each stalk a story, tall and proud,
Whispering secrets, soft yet loud.

Upon the breeze, a tale unfolds,
Of summer days and nights of gold.
In twilight's glow, all worries cease,
In sunlit dreams, we find our peace.

The sky, a canvas brushed with fire,
Ignites the hearts, lifts souls higher.
Wheat horizons stretch, vast and wide,
In golden seas, our hopes abide.

Through every sway, the light will dance,
Inviting all to take a chance.
To run through fields, to laugh and play,
In sunlit fantasies, we'll stay.

When shadows fall and stars align,
The memories of wheat will shine.
For in their beauty, we find grace,
In every golden, sunlit space.

# Pastel Dreams on Bending Stalks

Bending gently in the breeze,
Stalks of wheat sway with such ease.
In colors soft, a dreamlike scene,
Pastel hues in twilight sheen.

The air is kissed with fragrant sighs,
Where nature's beauty never lies.
Each blade a whisper of a tale,
As evening's light begins to pale.

With each turn, the colors blend,
Embracing twilight as a friend.
In shades of pink and lavender,
The wheat fields glow, a magic stir.

Time drifts by like a feathered sigh,
In this serene, enchanting sky.
These pastel dreams in nature's hold,
Are treasures gathered, worth more than gold.

As day succumbs to night's embrace,
The stars above take their place.
In bending stalks, we find delight,
Pastel dreams in the soft moonlight.

## The Celestial Sound of Wind on Wheat

A symphony in golden fields,
Where nature's heart its secret yields.
The wind, a voice, so soft, so clear,
Sings to the wheat, a song to hear.

Each whisper tells of days gone by,
As shadows dance beneath the sky.
A rustling hymn through every stalk,
The earth and air in gentle talk.

With every gust, a story flows,
Of sunlit skies and gentle snows.
The wheat waves back, a graceful sway,
In harmony, they weave the day.

As twilight casts a golden hue,
The wind's sweet tune feels ever true.
In fields, where time seems to stand still,
The air is filled with nature's will.

So listen close, let worries flee,
In the celestial symphony.
The sound of wind on golden seas,
Will fill your soul with tranquil ease.

# Celestial Gardens of Soft Twilight

In gardens where the shadows play,
The twilight whispers secrets low.
Stars awaken in the fading day,
A gentle breeze begins to blow.

Petals glisten in the dusky light,
Colors blend in a soft embrace.
Through the trees, the owls take flight,
Time slows down in this sacred space.

Dreamers gather on velvet grass,
Beneath the sky's enchanting dome.
In stillness, fleeting moments pass,
From this realm, they'll never roam.

Fires glow with a soft, warm hue,
Illuminating faces bright.
Stories shared, both old and new,
In these celestial gardens of light.

As night unfolds, the silence sings,
Echoes of laughter fill the air.
In twilight's arms, the spirit clings,
To magic found in moments rare.

# Moonlit Secrets of the Harvest Dance

Underneath the silver moon,
The fields of grain sway soft and low.
Harvest whispers, a gentle tune,
Inviting all to join the flow.

With laughter light, the children play,
As shadows stretch across the land.
Feet in rhythm, night turns to day,
Together, they make their stand.

Baskets filled with golden grain,
Sharing blessings, hearts all aligned.
The joy is pure, the love remains,
In every soul, a spark defined.

Twinkling stars above take flight,
Guardians of the night so grand.
In moonlit glow, the world feels right,
Bonded by a simple strand.

As dawn approaches, colors blend,
The harvest dance must soon retreat.
Yet in our hearts, the magic bends,
To memories that feel so sweet.

## Aura of Dreams in Amber Light

In the amber glow of fading day,
Visions dance in a dreamer's mind.
Colors swirl and take their play,
In whispers soft, the heart can find.

Fleeting moments in the twilight glow,
Time stands still, yet swiftly flows.
Underneath the stars, we know,
A gentle breeze through the garden blows.

Together in the golden haze,
We'll weave our tales of twilight grace.
Each breath holds magic in its gaze,
As time surrenders to this place.

Every shadow tells a story,
Of bright tomorrows yet to see.
With laughter, joy, and all its glory,
In this amber light, we're free.

The aura glows, alive with dreams,
Inviting hope to rise and soar.
In unity, our spirit gleams,
In the amber light forevermore.

# The Dance of Soft Breezes and Light

Beneath the glow of a painted sky,
The softly swaying trees entwine.
With every gust, the leaves reply,
In symphony, their dance divine.

Sunlight filters through branches wide,
Casting patterns on the ground.
Nature's rhythm as time does glide,
A tranquil pulse in harmony found.

Each petal sways, a gentle grace,
While whispers float on the softest breeze.
In these moments, our hearts embrace,
Embracing love, a soul's light tease.

The twilight brings a sweet refrain,
As crickets sing their softest song.
With every note, we feel no pain,
In the dance where we all belong.

Together under the setting sun,
We join the earth in joyous flight.
In unity, our hearts have won,
In the dance of soft breezes and light.

# Hues of Fantasy in Gentle Breezes

Whispers of colors, softly blend,
In twilight's embrace, dreams extend.
Each shade alive, a tale unfurls,
As breezes carry joy to worlds.

Chasing the sun, the clouds take flight,
Painting the sky with hues of light.
Petals flutter, laughter in air,
Magic blossoms, everywhere.

Gentle flows of cerulean streams,
Mingle with laughter, weave through dreams.
With every gust, new stories rise,
Under the watch of painted skies.

Softly the winds, they call and sway,
Inviting hearts to dance and play.
In every breath, a secret shared,
In fantasy's arms, all are bared.

So let us wander, hearts aglow,
In gentle breezes, let love grow.
With hues that shimmer, bright and true,
In this fantasy, me and you.

# Twilight's Dance with Golden Grains

Under the amber sky, we roam,
Fields of grains, a sun-kissed home.
Dancing shadows, in soft repose,
Twilight whispers, as night bestows.

Each stalk sways to a silent tune,
Bathed in silver from the moon.
With every rustle, secrets told,
In golden waves, the night unfolds.

Footsteps linger on the land,
Echoes of laughter, hand in hand.
As darkness falls, the fireflies gleam,
In twilight's dance, we share a dream.

Crickets sing, the stars awake,
A tapestry of light we make.
With every heartbeat, the night unchains,
A symphony played on golden grains.

In the hushed stillness, time suspends,
As nature's magic gently blends.
Together we weave, our hearts entwined,
In twilight's glow, our spirits find.

## Pastoral Reveries Under Moonlit Canopies

Fields stretch wide, in moonlit grace,
Where shadows play and dreams embrace.
Beneath the stars, the night unfolds,
In whispers soft, our story molds.

Gentle breezes breathe through trees,
Carrying tales from distant seas.
Each rustle speaks of love anew,
Under canopies, just me and you.

Silvery beams on dewy grass,
In this stillness, moments pass.
With every sigh and tender glance,
We lose ourselves in nature's dance.

Echoes of laughter in the night,
Wrapped in warmth of soft moonlight.
With hearts adorned in gentle light,
Together we dream till morning bright.

Pastoral scenes, in quiet dreams,
Where love awakens, or so it seems.
Beneath the arches where moments flow,
In moonlit canopies, our spirits grow.

# Ethereal Corners of Dusk

In corners where the shadows play,
The fading light bids farewell to day.
Soft hues blend where earth meets sky,
In ethereal realms, we learn to fly.

Each heartbeat echoes through the night,
Whispering secrets in fading light.
Stars awaken, a celestial sight,
As dusk embraces all in its flight.

Gentle breezes weave through the trees,
Carrying dreams like drifting leaves.
In twilight's arms, we find our way,
Through ethereal corners of the day.

Time pauses here, in this soft space,
In silence shared, we find our place.
With hands entwined, we softly tread,
In dusky corners where dreams are fed.

So let us linger in this embrace,
With stardust smiles upon our face.
In the magic that twilight brings,
We soar together on twilight's wings.

# The Grace of Plumed Meadows

In the meadows, blooms sway low,
Colors dancing in the soft glow.
Gentle breezes weave their song,
Nature's heartbeat, pure and strong.

Each petal whispers tales of old,
Of joys and secrets yet untold.
The sun dips low, a golden hue,
Plumed grasses kiss the morning dew.

Fields of gold stretch far and wide,
With every breath, the world inside.
A tranquil dance beneath the sky,
In this grace, our spirits fly.

Crickets chirp as daylight fades,
The night approaches, softly laid.
Under stars, a dreamlike trance,
Where silence offers sweet romance.

In plumed meadows, hearts unite,
A canvas painted by twilight.
In lush embrace, we find our place,
In nature's arms, a warm embrace.

# Whispers of Fantasia at Eventide

As dusk unfolds its velvet cloak,
Whispers dance, a tender stroke.
In the air, enchantments swirl,
A tapestry of dreams unfurl.

Softly glows the fading light,
Casting shadows, stealing night.
In the twilight, secrets blend,
Fantasia's song, a sweet commend.

Each star becomes a story told,
In silver dreams where hearts behold.
Whispers weave through branches high,
As the moon begins to sigh.

Magic glistens on the stream,
Where fireflies ignite the dream.
In the quiet, wishes soar,
Unraveling tales forevermore.

At eventide, we dare to drift,
To chase the light, a perfect gift.
With open hearts and open minds,
In this realm, the joy unwinds.

# Soft Lights in Dreamy Pastures

In pastures wide, the soft lights gleam,
Beneath the moon, we softly dream.
Gentle whispers fill the air,
With every breath, a quiet prayer.

Stars above begin to hum,
Calling forth the night to come.
Shadows dance in the silver glow,
Where secret tales of twilight flow.

Each blade of grass, a story sings,
A world alive with wondrous things.
Bathed in hues of azure and gold,
In dreamy pastures, we are bold.

Through fields of light, we wander free,
Lost in dreams of what could be.
With hearts aglow, we will explore,
Soft lights beckon us to soar.

In this embrace, the world feels right,
As we chase the fading light.
A gentle wish upon a star,
In dreamy pastures, near and far.

## Whimsy in Starlit Cornfields

In the cornfields, shadows play,
Whimsy blooms at close of day.
Under stars that brightly gleam,
We dance along the edge of dreams.

With rustling leaves, the stories flow,
Echoed laughter mingles low.
Moonlit paths weave through the stalks,
Where magic whispers, softly talks.

Tiny creatures join the fun,
In the glow of the evening sun.
Adventure calls in hushed delight,
Guided by the silvery light.

Winding trails lead us so near,
To the heart where joy is clear.
Through whispers of the night we roam,
In starlit cornfields, we find home.

With every step, a new surprise,
Beneath the vast, enchanting skies.
In whimsy's grasp, our spirits soar,
In starlit cornfields, forevermore.

# Golden Whispers in Twilight

Golden hues dance in the night,
Where dreams take flight with delight.
The stars awaken, softly glow,
Whispering tales from long ago.

The breeze carries secrets profound,
As shadows of twilight surround.
Moments held in a gentle sigh,
Underneath the vast, open sky.

Nature breathes in tender sighs,
As the sun bids the world goodbye.
With every heartbeat, time stands still,
In the twilight's enchanting thrill.

Echoes of laughter fade away,
As night claims the warmth of day.
Golden whispers, sweet and clear,
Sing to the heart, drawing near.

In the silence, dreams are spun,
Under the gaze of the lone sun.
Each whispered thought, a glowing spark,
Guiding lost souls through the dark.

## Dreams Woven in Amber Fields

Amber grains sway with the breeze,
Whispers of comfort, secrets tease.
Fields aglow in the setting sun,
Where the day and night become one.

Underneath the vast, soft skies,
The world inhales with gentle sighs.
Dreams emerge, fragile, yet bold,
Stories of life waiting to be told.

Golden threads weave through the air,
Catch the sunlight, dance without care.
Every heartbeat wrapped in light,
As day fades into starry night.

Echoes of laughter in the lanes,
Filling the air amid the grains.
These moments like treasures will hold,
Dreams woven in amber, pure gold.

As the twilight embraces the land,
The heart finds peace, a soothing hand.
In fields of warm memories and grace,
Dreams are alive in this sacred space.

# Serenades of Celestial Pastures

In pastures wide, the stars ignite,
With melodies echoing through the night.
Celestial wonders dance above,
Serenades sung by the clouds of love.

Each whisper carries a gentle breeze,
Across the hills, through swaying trees.
Moonlit paths where shadows play,
Guide wandering souls at end of day.

Stars align in a cosmic vein,
Singing stories of loss and gain.
The heart beats in the softest glow,
A serenade known to only a few.

Nature hums its timeless refrain,
In every heart, joy and pain.
Celestial pastures call us near,
To embrace the night without fear.

With each note, the universe sighs,
Encouraging eyes to look at the skies.
In the serenade's softest charms,
Life is held in celestial arms.

# Enchanted Fields at Dusk

Dusk settles soft on the lush ground,
In enchanted fields, peace is found.
Colors blend in a magical hue,
Where dreams linger, old and new.

Whispers of grass beneath the feet,
The heart finds rhythm, calm and sweet.
Fading sunlight wraps the trees,
Cradling secrets in the breeze.

Twilight casts its gentle spell,
In every shadow, stories dwell.
With every breath, the earth awakens,
In the stillness, a heart overtaken.

Soft laughter rides the evening tides,
As nature's beauty softly abides.
In enchanted corridors of gold,
Every moment feels new and bold.

With stars bursting forth in their flight,
The world transforms in tranquil light.
In the dance of dusk, we are free,
Embracing the night's soft reverie.

# Tales Told by Golden Stems

In fields where golden stems stand tall,
Whispers of the wind do call.
Each leaf a story, a secret spun,
Underneath the warming sun.

Beneath the sky, so vast and wide,
The tales of nature cannot hide.
With every rustle, a voice so clear,
Binding us to memories dear.

As harvest moons begin to rise,
The echoes dance like fireflies.
With every heartbeat, life anew,
In golden fields, our dreams accrue.

Time flows gently like a stream,
In the glow of twilight's beam.
The stories weave through every hue,
In nature's cradle, love rings true.

So let us wander, hand in hand,
Through these tales, forever grand.
For in each golden stem we find,
The heart of life, beautifully entwined.

# Murmurs of Unicorns in Sunlit Valleys

In sunlit valleys, soft and bright,
Murmurs float on gentle light.
Unicorns dance with grace divine,
In harmony with nature's line.

With every hoofbeat on the grass,
Magic stirs as shadows pass.
Through wildflowers, they gently tread,
Whispering tales of the ancient red.

Their horns aglow with colors rare,
Merging dreams with fragrant air.
In secret glades, where wonders grow,
The murmurs rise, a soothing flow.

As sunbeams kiss the hills so high,
These creatures wander, spirits nigh.
With every glance, enchantments sway,
In the valley's heart, they softly play.

Let us cherish these moments bright,
Where unicorns roam in pure delight.
In their murmurings, we'll find our way,
Through sunlit valleys, come what may.

# The Whispering Grain and Shining Sky

The golden grain sways to the beat,
A symphony of nature, oh so sweet.
Under a sky of azure dreams,
Life flows like the sun's warm beams.

Whispers echo through fields of gold,
Stories of the brave and bold.
Each stalk a guardian of the past,
In every grain, a future cast.

Clouds drift lazily through the air,
Painting pictures with utmost care.
The sun bows low, a gentle sigh,
As evening wraps the day nearby.

With arms outstretched, the world we greet,
In the dance of nature, hearts entreat.
Together we're woven, strong and free,
In whispering grains, we find our glee.

So let us linger where the wild winds play,
In the embrace of the twilight's sway.
For in this moment, together we shine,
With whispering grain and sky divine.

# Radiant Colors in Soothing Sighs

In twilight's glow, colors blend and rise,
Radiant hues in soothing sighs.
The world transforms in gentle light,
Painting stories that feel just right.

With every stroke of nature's hand,
A masterpiece across the land.
Soft whispers float on evening breeze,
Dancing with the rustling leaves.

Above, the stars begin to gleam,
Mirroring our deepest dream.
As night descends, our hearts unite,
In radiant colors, pure delight.

The moon serenades the silent sea,
Bathing all in tranquility.
Each sigh a promise, soft and true,
A lullaby for me and you.

So let us cherish this peaceful night,
Where colors shine in soft twilight.
For in soothing sighs, love will find,
A canvas painted, heart and mind.

# Harmony of Grains and Stars

In fields where golden grains do sway,
The stars above begin to play.
A gentle breeze whispers delight,
As day surrenders to the night.

The moon, a guardian so bright,
Watches over the earth's sweet flight.
Each shadow dances, soft and free,
Bound in nature's harmony.

The dew-kissed leaves shimmer and gleam,
Mirroring the celestial dream.
Night paints the canvas, dark and vast,
In this moment, we are cast.

The whispers of the nighttime air,
Blend with secrets we can share.
Each grain, a story told anew,
In the glow of starlit hue.

So let us weave this tale of peace,
Where night and day find sweet release.
In every heart, the echoes play,
Of grains and stars, a soft ballet.

# Celestial Echoes in Amber Fields

Beneath a sky of endless grace,
Amber fields in sunlight's embrace.
Whispers rise like dreams on the wing,
Nature's hymn is what we sing.

Clouds drift softly, white and bright,
Mirroring the heart's pure light.
In every rustle, stories old,
Of love and life waiting to be told.

The horizon kisses the day's end,
As shadows stretch, our hopes ascend.
The stars will dance in twilight's glow,
In amber fields where dreams will flow.

Each heartbeat echoes through the night,
A rhythm sweet, a pure delight.
In harmony with earth and sky,
Where whispers of the past still fly.

Together, we'll hold this sacred ground,
In these fields, our peace is found.
With every step, we shall ignite,
Celestial echoes, pure and bright.

## Rainbow Rhapsody Over Silken Grasses

In glades where silken grasses sway,
A rainbow paints the skies in play.
Colors burst in joyful cheer,
Nature's canvas, vivid and clear.

Each hue a note in sweet refrain,
A symphony that breaks the rain.
Together in this vibrant light,
We find the magic of pure sight.

Butterflies dance on gentle breeze,
Carving paths through trees with ease.
The world becomes a vibrant dream,
As sunbeams and dewdrops gleam.

Every petal, a whisper soft,
Carries tales of when they loft.
In fields of green, our spirits soar,
With nature's rhythm at our core.

So let us twirl in joy today,
With rainbows guiding our bright way.
In silken grasses, love confides,
In rhapsody where beauty hides.

# Starlit Melodies in Verdant Valleys

In valleys lush where shadows play,
Starlit whispers grace the day.
Beneath the vast and starry dome,
Nature sings, calling us home.

Each twinkling light, a lullaby,
Softly weaving through the sky.
The nightingale joins in the song,
In harmony where we belong.

The rustle of leaves, a tender peace,
In moonlit glades where sorrows cease.
The world transforms in twilight's glow,
As starlit dreams begin to flow.

With every breeze, a tale unfolds,
Of timeless love and dreams retold.
In verdant valleys, we unite,
Lost in starlit melodies tonight.

As stars align and hearts entwine,
In the quiet, pure, divine.
Together we will roam afar,
In the magic of a glowing star.

# Mystical Whispers in Sundown Glade

In the glade where shadows play,
Whispers twirl and dance away.
Leaves like secrets softly sigh,
As twilight paints the evening sky.

Crickets weave their gentle song,
While dusky hues begin to throng.
A breeze carries tales of lore,
Echoes of what came before.

Golden rays break through the trees,
A hint of magic in the breeze.
Footsteps hush on mossy ground,
As nature's secrets swirl around.

Stars awaken, one by one,
A symphony has just begun.
In the silence, hearts abide,
On this mystical evening ride.

The world transforms in twilight's clutch,
Realms unknown that gently touch.
Lost in wonder, time does fade,
In the whispers of the glade.

# Celestial Melody on Sunflower Trails

On trails where sunflowers stand tall,
Their golden heads heed nature's call.
Bees hum softly, weaving tunes,
Underneath the smiling moon.

A breeze might sway the leafy greens,
In fields adorned with vibrant sheens.
Every petal tells a tale,
Of summer's grace, a fragrant trail.

Clouds drift slowly, dreamily by,
Kissed by rays of a lavender sky.
Harmony lingers in the air,
As colors blend without a care.

Evening descends, a velvet sheet,
In the quiet, hearts skip a beat.
Dancing lights from fireflies spark,
A celestial dance in the dark.

Through sunflower trails, love blooms bright,
Wrapped in warmth of waning light.
A melody of dusk we chase,
In every whisper, nature's grace.

# Daybreak's Brush over Golden Stalks

When the dawn begins to rise,
Painting gold across the skies.
Fields stretch wide in morning's glow,
As whispers of the night let go.

Birds take flight, their songs alight,
With dreams from the stars, taking flight.
Golden stalks sway in the breeze,
Nature wakes with gentle ease.

A palette rich with hues so bright,
Each blade of grass kissed by light.
The world awakens, fresh and new,
As daybreak bathes the ground in dew.

The sun climbs high, a ball of fire,
Lighting hearts with pure desire.
In this moment, life does sing,
Renewed joy that mornings bring.

Through verdant paths, new wonders call,
Each step resonates, we feel it all.
In the warmth of day's embrace,
Nature's beauty, a sacred space.

# Harmonics of Dusk on Painted Skies

As dusk arrives, the colors blend,
The day surrenders, night ascends.
Brush strokes of lavender and rose,
In painted skies, beauty glows.

Gentle whispers in the air,
Nature stirs with a tender flair.
The stars prepare their nightly show,
While shadows dance and breezes flow.

Moonlight drapes the world in grace,
A silver glow on every face.
The symphony of night begins,
As twilight wraps the earth like skin.

Crickets join the evening choir,
In harmony, they never tire.
Each note a thread in night's embrace,
Sewn together in perfect space.

In this moment, hearts take flight,
Lost in the magic of the night.
Harmonics of dusk, sweetly sigh,
Where dreams take root and time slips by.

# A Tapestry of Glimmering Dreams

In the quiet night sky, stars weep,
Threads of silver, the wishes we keep.
Moonlight dances on ripples of thought,
Weaving tales of all that time forgot.

Colors blend in a hushed embrace,
As shadows swirl, a soft, gentle chase.
Each shimmering hope, a whisper of grace,
In a tapestry born of a dreamer's space.

Time drifts like a feather on the breeze,
Carrying secrets, the heart's sweet pleas.
Beneath the vastness, we lie in awe,
Capturing fragments of wonder's raw law.

Crickets sing soft, a lullaby's tune,
Nurtured by starlight, beneath a bright moon.
Glimmers of fate, in patterns align,
In the tapestry woven, our stories intertwine.

So here we rest, as the night unfolds,
In this canvas of dreams, our future holds.
With every thread, a promise we weave,
In the glow of our hopes, we believe.

# The Dance of Colors in Whispered Hours

Upon the canvas, hues collide,
With every stroke, our hearts confide.
Sunset's blush in amber breeze,
Soft whispers carried through the trees.

Here in twilight's gentle guise,
Colors bloom beneath the skies.
Violet shadows merge with gold,
In whispered hours, their stories told.

Brushes sway like lovers' sighs,
Painting moments, where time flies.
A swirl of dreams on a fading light,
In the realm of dusk, we find delight.

Each hue a memory, a lingering glance,
Captured in the night's soft dance.
As stars ignite the painted sea,
The colors sing, and we are free.

So let us revel in this art,
Where colors bind the world's pure heart.
In whispered moments, we shall find,
The dance of colors, forever entwined.

# Dusk's Embrace on Timid Flowers

As daylight fades, the shadows creep,
Dusk wraps softly, a tender sweep.
Petals sigh in the evening's breath,
In twilight's hold, they flirt with death.

The sky dips low in hues of rose,
Close to the earth, a gentle pose.
Timid flowers, in silence, bloom,
Embraced by dusk, they shun the gloom.

Whispers of night cradle their dreams,
As soft as the sound of distant streams.
The world grows quiet, a soft refrain,
In dusk's embrace, we feel no pain.

Beneath the stars, they softly sway,
In the calm of night, they find their way.
With every sigh, they share their plight,
In a dance with dusk, they seek the light.

So let us linger in the hour,
Where timid flowers find their power.
In the twilight's hush, we too must find,
The beauty in night's gentle bind.

# Fables Carved in Mellow Light

In the glow of lanterns, stories breathe,
Fables whispered, the night we weave.
Carved in shadows, the tales take flight,
Guided softly by mellow light.

Each flicker tells of ancient lore,
Of lost kingdoms and heart's rich core.
Through the haze of dreams, we gather near,
To echo the voices that we hold dear.

Every whisper dances in the air,
Carving moments with tender care.
Magical sights in the soft twilight,
Unraveling fables, hidden from sight.

The embers fade, but the tales remain,
Carved in the memory, like a sweet refrain.
Under the stars, we gather close,
Sharing our dreams, a heartfelt dose.

So let us listen, and let us roam,
In the stories of light, we find our home.
For in every fable, there's a spark,
Illuminating life in the gentle dark.

# Magic Lingers where the Grains Sway

Golden fields stretch far and wide,
Where secrets of the earth reside.
Breezes dance with whispers light,
In twilight's glow, the stars ignite.

Sunsets paint the sky in hues,
As shadows blend, the heart renews.
Crickets sing their evening song,
In nature's arms, where we belong.

Each grain sways with silent grace,
Holding stories time can't erase.
The gentle rustle, nature's tune,
Beneath the watchful, silver moon.

In every shift, there's magic spun,
A hint of dreams, a trace of fun.
Together, grains and dreams entwine,
In this enchanted space, divine.

So let us linger, hand in hand,
In fields of gold, a timeless land.
For here, in whispers soft and low,
The seeds of magic ever grow.

# Embracing Dreams Under Pastel Veils

A canvas stretched of softest pink,
Where twilight's shadows gently wink.
Pastel hues embrace the night,
As dreams take flight on whispered light.

Clouds sail by in lavender streams,
Stars awash in golden dreams.
We gather wishes like the dew,
A tapestry in shades so true.

In this embrace, our hearts align,
With every breath, the stars we dine.
Time slows down as moments blend,
In pastel veils, our spirits mend.

Let whispers guide us through the dark,
As stardust weaves a glowing spark.
In every shade, a story told,
Each dream a thread of shimmering gold.

So hold my hand, let's drift away,
Beneath these skies, we'll choose to stay.
In pastel veils, our spirits soar,
Embracing dreams forevermore.

# Echoes of Color in Whispering Fields

Amidst the blooms, bright colors call,
Echoing softly, a vibrant thrall.
Each petal sways in rhythmic grace,
In whispering fields, our dreams embrace.

Rays of sunshine weave their spells,
As nature's story gently dwells.
Colors bloom in every glance,
Awakening hearts to nature's dance.

Butterflies flutter, bright and free,
In this realm of vivid glee.
Echoes of laughter, joy untold,
In fields of color, tales unfold.

With every breeze, the colors sing,
A symphony that hearts can bring.
In whispers deep, we'll find our way,
Through echoes bright, come what may.

So let the fields inspire our souls,
With every hue, our spirit rolls.
In this canvas, we find the real,
Echoes of color, the heart's appeal.

# A Harmonious Blend of Dawn and Dusk

The sky awakens, soft and bright,
As dawn emerges, chasing night.
Colors blend in a radiant hue,
A dance of light, a world anew.

Birds sing sweetly in morning's glow,
As shadows linger, slow and low.
Each moment whispers tales unspoken,
In dawn's embrace, hearts feel unbroken.

As day unfolds, time starts to wane,
The golden hour, a gentle reign.
Dusk arrives with a velvet sigh,
Painting dreams in the evening sky.

Stars begin to twinkle bright,
As day surrenders to the night.
A harmonious blend, a perfect tune,
In twilight's arms, we'll find the moon.

So let us dance through dawn and dusk,
In every moment, a touch of trust.
For life's a melody sweet and true,
A harmonious blend, me and you.

# Pastel Skies and Gentle Breezes

Pastel hues greet the dawn light,
Whispers of dreams take their flight.
Clouds like candy drift away,
Soften the warmth of the day.

Gentle breezes kiss my skin,
Carrying laughter, where to begin?
Nature dances, a serene bliss,
Moments like this, I never miss.

Colors blend in a radiant glow,
Painting the world in a tender flow.
With each sigh, the heart expands,
Wrapped in beauty, life understands.

In this haven, time stands still,
Filling my soul, a quiet thrill.
Beneath the skies, a canvas wide,
Where hope and joy always reside.

So let me linger in this space,
Embraced by light, a soft embrace.
With pastel skies, my spirit flies,
Among the clouds, my heart replies.

# Echoes of Shimmering Hope

In the quiet of the night,
Whispers of dreams take flight.
Stars like jewels, bright and clear,
Echoes of hope, always near.

Silver linings chase the dark,
Illuminating every spark.
Promises dance in moonlight's glow,
Guiding hearts where courage flows.

Each heartbeat sings a song,
Reminding us where we belong.
In shadows deep, we find our way,
With shimmering hope, we won't sway.

Every doubt begins to fade,
As bright futures dance, unafraid.
In the silence, strength abounds,
Echoes of hope, the heart resounds.

So let the stars weave their tales,
With every breath, hope prevails.
In the calm, we find our way,
Embracing dreams, come what may.

# Fields of Gold in Starry Nights

In fields of gold, the moonlight spills,
Whispers of night provide sweet thrills.
Waves of grain softly sway,
Crickets sing in gentle play.

Amid the stars, the heavens shine,
Glimmers of hope, so divine.
Every breath, a treasure found,
In this beauty, hearts are bound.

The breeze carries secrets of old,
Stories of dreams, timeless and bold.
Under the sky, so vast and true,
Fields of gold, where love renews.

With each step on the earthen path,
Nature's warmth, a soothing bath.
In the silence, peace unfolds,
Embracing life, in fields of gold.

So let us wander through the night,
Guided by stars, our hearts alight.
In fields of gold, we find our home,
Underneath the night, we roam.

# The Unicorn's Gentle Embrace

In dreams so soft, a unicorn waits,
With a shimmer of light, it captivates.
A gentle spirit, pure and wise,
Its grace reflected in starry skies.

With every step, magic unfurls,
Whispers of peace in a world of pearls.
Hooves that dance on the silver ground,
In its presence, joy is found.

A friendship born from spirit's flight,
Guiding hearts through the darkest night.
With every nudge, worries erase,
Forever cherished in its embrace.

With silken mane and eyes so bright,
It leads us into the soft twilight.
In the stillness, dreams do weave,
In the unicorn's love, we believe.

So let us journey, side by side,
With magical grace as our guide.
In this embrace, we come alive,
With the unicorn's love, we thrive.

## Illusions of Gold in Dusk's Embrace

The sun sinks low, a fiery hue,
Whispers of night creep softly through.
Golden fields bathe in twilight's glow,
Yet shadows lengthen, as whispers grow.

Hearts dance lightly, lost in the phase,
Chasing sparks in the warm twilight haze.
Dreams weave tales of glitter and seam,
In dusk's embrace, we drift and dream.

## Melodies of the Charmed Horizon

A breeze carries tunes of the night,
Notes twinkle bright, a starry flight.
Symphonies born from the moving trees,
Charmed horizon, hums with the breeze.

Each moment lingers, a song's sweet grace,
Nature's rhythm finds its place.
In every sigh, a melody wafts,
Painting the air with gentle crafts.

## Celestial Peace in Fields of Dreams

Under a sky where the stardust swirls,
Fields of dreams unfurl like pearls.
The moonlight bathes each sleeping crest,
In celestial peace, our worries rest.

Gentle whispers of nightbirds sing,
Crickets join in, a symphonic ring.
Time slows down, the world stands still,
In tranquil fields, we taste the thrill.

## Fantasies in the Shade of Grain

Rustling whispers through amber blades,
Where sunlight plays and laughter wades.
In shadows long, where dreams lie deep,
Fantasies awaken from their sleep.

Golden whispers near the brook's edge,
Childhood enchantments, a joyous pledge.
The air is thick with secrets untold,
In the shade of grain, love unfolds.

# Chasing Shadows of Mythical Beasts

In the twilight's gentle hush,
Whispers ride the evening's brush.
Figures dance in moonlit glow,
Legends play, their secrets flow.

Fleeting forms in forest deep,
Guardians of the night that keep.
Eyes aglow with ancient fire,
Stirring hearts with wild desire.

A dragon's roar, the phoenix's flight,
Echoes of a timeless night.
Bound by tales of yore's embrace,
Chasing shadows in a sacred space.

The centaur's grace, the griffin's might,
Heroes forged in dream and light.
Each pursuit a silent quest,
In this dance, we find our rest.

As dawn breaks through the veil of mist,
We bid farewell to the moon's kiss.
Yet in our hearts, forever dwell,
The shadows of the beastly spell.

# Silken Strands of Sunlit Harmony

In the meadow, sunlight pours,
Threads of gold on gentle shores.
Nature hums a soft refrain,
Weaving joy where peace is plain.

Breezes carry sweet perfume,
Wildflowers dance in nature's bloom.
Colors blend in joyous throng,
Nature's voice, a vibrant song.

Amidst the trees, a chorus sings,
Birds take flight on silver wings.
Each note a love, a tender grace,
Wrapped in warmth, a sweet embrace.

Through the fields, the children run,
Chasing shadows, bathed in fun.
Echoes linger in the air,
Moments captured, pure and rare.

As daylight wanes and stars ignite,
We hold dear the day's delight.
In silken strands, our hearts align,
Together weaves a love divine.

## Lullabies of the Dappled Dawn

Morning breaks with gentle sighs,
A tapestry of painted skies.
Birds serenade the waking light,
Softly whispering dreams take flight.

Sunbeams dance on dewy grass,
Waking life as shadows pass.
Each leaf shimmers, a gleaming sight,
Nature's lullabies, pure delight.

The brook babbles with tender grace,
Cradling thoughts in its embrace.
Awakening the sleeping earth,
Celebrating a brand new birth.

Frogs croon low in harmony,
A chorus of simplicity.
Gentle breezes stir the trees,
Spreading calm like whispered pleas.

As the sun ascends so bright,
We cherish every golden light.
In the heart of this serene dawn,
Lullabies of joy are drawn.

# Melodies in the Warmth of Grain

Fields of gold beneath the sky,
Waves of grain as whispers fly.
Rustling softly in the breeze,
Nature sings with gentle ease.

Harvest dreams, a bountiful song,
Where we all find we belong.
Hands embrace the earth's warm skin,
Melodies that stir within.

Midst the stalks, the children play,
Laughter brightens up the day.
Frosty nights yield to dawn's bloom,
Fruitful fields dispel the gloom.

An old oak stands with wisdom grand,
Roots deep in this cherished land.
Its branches cradle all that's known,
Nurturing seeds that have grown.

As the season turns and sways,
We celebrate in countless ways.
Melodies in the warmth we gain,
Bound by love, we feel no pain.

# Enchantment of Twilight Corners

Shadows dance where whispers play,
Twilight drapes the end of day.
Stars awaken, shy and bright,
In the corners, hearts take flight.

Breezes hum a secret tune,
As daylight bows to gentle moon.
Laughter lingers, soft and clear,
In twilight's embrace, we draw near.

Petals close, the world slows down,
Dreams take shape in dusky brown.
Mysteries in silence dwell,
Tales are spun as nighttime fell.

Rustling leaves and crickets' song,
In this magic, we belong.
Glimmers of a world so wide,
In twilight corners, journeys bide.

Eyes aflame, with wonder's spark,
In the hush, we leave a mark.
Beneath the sky, our spirits soar,
In enchantment, we crave more.

# Horizons Painted with Celestial Light

Beyond the hills, the colors bloom,
Brushstrokes fill the evening gloom.
Gold and blue begin to blend,
As day and night start to mend.

Skyward dreams dance overhead,
With whispers of the stars long dead.
A canvas stretched, beyond our sight,
Horizons drip with pure delight.

Clouds like thoughts drift and sway,
In the twilight, they softly play.
Each hue a story, soft yet bright,
Shadows cast by fading light.

Waves of dusk with whispers keep,
As colors blush and softly seep.
Transitioning from day to night,
Horizons shimmer, pure and bright.

Beneath the stars, a silent vow,
Nature's promise seen right now.
In frames of dreams, we take our flight,
Where horizons dance with celestial light.

# Songs of Tranquility in Amber Fields

Golden waves beneath the sun,
In amber fields, our hearts are one.
Whispers float upon the breeze,
As nature sings with gentle ease.

Clouds drift lazily on high,
Painted dreams across the sky.
Sunset's glow wraps all in warmth,
In silence, we find our calm heart.

Each blade of grass a story told,
In hues of gold and warmth unfold.
Tranquil moments, softly speak,
In amber fields, the strong and weak.

Footsteps tread on softened earth,
Echoes of our shared worth.
With every sigh, the world feels new,
As serenity flows, pure and true.

Songs of sunsets, bright and clear,
Envelop souls who wander here.
In amber fields where echoes blend,
Tranquility finds a soothing friend.

## Hidden Realms of Grainy Delight

Beneath the surface, worlds abide,
In whispers soft, they try to hide.
Grains of sand and time entwined,
In hidden realms of every mind.

Shimmering grains with tales of old,
Secrets of the sea retold.
History's echo, barely seen,
In the depths, where dreams convene.

With every step, a gentle sway,
Footprints left in fleeting play.
Mirages tease the wandering eyes,
In grainy realms where magic lies.

Sunset glimmers on the shore,
In hushed tones, they call for more.
Among the dunes, a whispered flight,
In hidden realms of grainy delight.

Together we weave tales untold,
In sun-kissed sand and moonlit gold.
With hearts aligned, we take our chance,
In these realms, our spirits dance.

# Fairy Stories in Grassy Coils

In meadows green where fairies play,
Whispers dance in light of day.
Softly they weave their tales of old,
Secrets in the grass unfold.

Butterflies flit with laughter near,
Bringing joy, erasing fear.
Each petal holds a story bright,
Magic glows in morning light.

Waving leaves in gentle breeze,
Nature sings with such great ease.
Every shadow, every sound,
Entwined in stories yet unbound.

Little hearts with dreams take flight,
Underneath the starry night.
In this realm of lush delight,
Fairy tales take wing in flight.

With every breeze the tales arise,
Spinning softly like the skies.
In grassy coils they lovingly dwell,
Echoing their timeless spell.

# The Dance of Grain in Colorful Skies

Fields of gold beneath the blue,
Glisten bright in morning dew.
Grains of wheat like waves align,
In the breeze, a dance divine.

Sunset paints the world with fire,
Nature's beauty, hearts inspire.
Wind sweeps low, the grains will sway,
In the dusk, they dance and play.

Colors burst in vibrant hues,
Every shade, a tale to choose.
Underneath the broad expanse,
Life unfolds in gentle dance.

Crickets chirp the night's soft tune,
Over fields beneath the moon.
Waves of grain in shadows rise,
Choreographed by evening skies.

In this vast and rolling sea,
Nature's art is wild and free.
With every grain, history rhymes,
Dancing gently through the climes.

# Twilight's Serenade on Starlit Hills

Whispers of the evening breeze,
Crickets sing among the trees.
Stars appear, a silver thread,
Twilight lingers, dreams are bred.

Hills embrace the gentle night,
Where shadows merge with soft moonlight.
Each star a note in night's ballet,
Serenading the end of day.

Fireflies flicker, give their cheer,
Lighting paths to places near.
Underneath the silent bloom,
Nature hums a soft perfume.

In the calm, the world breathes slow,
Harmonies of twilight grow.
Magic dances in the air,
Every heart finds freedom there.

With each breath, the moments twine,
Life's sweet song in the divine.
On starlit hills, the dreams take flight,
In twilight's serenade of light.

# Sunlight Filtering through Wheat Waves

Morning sun in golden streams,
Waves of wheat fulfill their dreams.
Gentle rays, a warm embrace,
Nature's bounty, pure grace.

Fields await the light's soft kiss,
In this moment, find your bliss.
Rustling whispers, joy in sight,
Sunlight dances, pure delight.

Shadows play on golden blades,
As the day slowly cascades.
Every grain a story spun,
Underneath the watching sun.

In this symphony of light,
Hope awakens with the bright.
Waves of wheat, a gentle sigh,
Cherishing the endless sky.

Nature breathes with every sway,
In the warmth, let's laugh and play.
Sunlight filtering with such grace,
In this world, we find our place.

# Shadows of Enchantment in Wheatfields

Whispers of wind, in golden waves,
Dancing through stalks that sunlight saves.
Under a sky of azure bright,
Mysteries blend in soft daylight.

Shadows stretch long, as day meets night,
Secrets unfold in fading light.
A tapestry woven from dreams untold,
Nature's embrace, a sight to behold.

Footsteps wander on paths so rare,
Guided by whispers of the air.
Wheat rustles softly, a soothing sound,
In this enchanted space, peace is found.

Beneath the horizon where shadows play,
Golden fields dance, then slowly sway.
Heartbeats sync with the rhythm of earth,
In this sacred place, we find our worth.

In twilight's glow, a gentle sigh,
Stars awaken in the velvet sky.
Memories linger as day takes flight,
In wheatfields' shadows, the world feels right.

# Frosted Dreams of the Ethereal Realm

In a frozen world where silence reigns,
Glistening crystals adorn the plains.
Whispers of frost in the still of night,
Dreams take shape in shimmering light.

Soft sighs echo through the chilly air,
Breath becomes mist, swirling with care.
Stars twinkle bright in a canvas of blue,
Guiding the wanderers' hearts anew.

A symphony plays on the frostbitten leaves,
Nature's sweet song, the spirit believes.
Crispness envelops with each gentle gust,
In this ethereal realm, we find trust.

Snowflakes descend in delicate dance,
Holding soft beauty in their romance.
In the hush of the night, our dreams take flight,
Guided by visions that shimmer so bright.

In frozen wonder, we lose track of time,
Each moment a treasure, each breath a rhyme.
Frosted dreams wrap us in their embrace,
In the ethereal realm, we find our place.

# Gentle Rhapsody in Prismatic Fields

In fields of color where rainbows gleam,
Nature guides us, weaving a dream.
Petals unfold in a soft ballet,
Dancing with light in a graceful sway.

The air is sweet with perfume so light,
A gentle rhapsody, pure delight.
Butterflies flit through the vibrant blooms,
Each one a note in nature's tunes.

Golden sunbeams kiss the land,
Caressing flowers with a tender hand.
In this paradise, hearts intertwine,
Lost in the beauty, we know we shine.

Verdant green meets the azure skies,
A canvas painted with no goodbyes.
Every glance a melody, every sigh,
In prismatic fields, the soul learns to fly.

As the sun dips low, colors blend and fade,
The day whispers secrets that never degrade.
In the hush of twilight, our hearts take heed,
In this gentle rhapsody, we are freed.

# Hushed Tones of Twilight's Glow

When twilight descends with a hush so deep,
Dreams weave softly through the veil we keep.
Stars begin to sparkle, a delicate show,
Painting the sky in twilight's glow.

Whispers of dusk wrap the world in peace,
A moment of calm where worries cease.
Silhouettes whisper in shadows that play,
As day whispers secrets, fading away.

Crickets sing softly, the night takes flight,
Moonlight caresses the edges of night.
In this serene hour, hearts find their way,
Guided by dreams that gently sway.

Time slips away like grains of sand,
In twilight's embrace, we silently stand.
Each breath a promise, each moment a vow,
In hushed tones of magic, we live in the now.

As stars light the canvas of midnight's breath,
We find ourselves dancing, defying death.
In this tranquil rapture, we feel the flow,
Embraced by the beauty of twilight's glow.

## Dreamweaver's Touch on a Cornfield

In golden waves the corn does dance,
Beneath the sky, a dreamlike trance.
Whispers of wind through stalks do play,
As daylight fades to end the day.

Silhouettes stretch against the light,
A canvas drawn in hues so bright.
Breath of summer, soft and sweet,
Nature's pulse, a rhythmic beat.

Stars awaken in twilight's embrace,
Casting their glow on this sacred space.
Each ear of corn, a story told,
In tender whispers, dreams unfold.

Moonlight drapes a silver cloak,
On swaying fields, a gentle stroke.
Silent wishes ride the breeze,
Carried far with perfect ease.

Awaiting dawn's warm, tender kiss,
In cornfields, find your secret bliss.
The dreamer wanders, heart in hand,
In this vast and golden land.

# Glittering Hues of a Gentle Night

Beneath the stars, the world ignites,
With colors dancing through the nights.
A tranquil hush, a soft reprieve,
Where dreams emerge and hearts believe.

The moonlight spills on dew-kissed leaves,
A magic realm where silence weaves.
Shadows play in an endless waltz,
In this embrace, the heart somersaults.

Velvet skies adorned with light,
Bring forth tales of sheer delight.
Each twinkling star, a wish set free,
In gentle night, just you and me.

A breeze whispers in hushed tones,
While crickets serenade in drones.
The world is calm, the time stands still,
As dreams unfold with quiet thrill.

Glimmers of hope in every gleam,
Softest whispers echo a dream.
In glittering hues, take flight tonight,
For in this stillness, hearts feel light.

## Daydreams Spun in Golden Threads

With morning light, the world awakes,
In whispers soft, the day remakes.
Daydreams dance within the mind,
In golden threads, the heart unbinds.

Fields of barley, gleaming bright,
Touched by softly spilling light.
Every shadow, every shade,
A tapestry through time is laid.

Thoughts take flight on gentle wings,
In quiet moments, life gently sings.
Laughter bubbles, joy unspun,
The magic of day has just begun.

Through the hours, the colors flow,
In swirls of amber, they brightly glow.
Each fleeting moment, pure delight,
In daydreams spun, we find our flight.

As dusk approaches, whispers blend,
In golden dreams, we find our friend.
Hold tight the visions, let them grow,
For in this space, our hopes shall glow.

## The Elegance of Color in Quietude

In tranquil spaces, colors blend,
Each gentle hue, a graceful friend.
Whispers soft, a painter's touch,
Nature's art, it means so much.

Lavender skies with rosy tints,
A quiet peace, the heart convinces.
Through emerald leaves, the sunlight spills,
A symphony of soft, sweet thrills.

Gentle breezes carry sound,
Of rustling leaves upon the ground.
Every moment, a brush of grace,
In quietude, we find our place.

The elegance of twilight's glare,
Wraps the world in tender care.
As colors wane, the stars appear,
In calmness felt, we draw them near.

Hold to the beauty, breathe it in,
In the silence, let dreams begin.
With every shade, a story spun,
In quietude, we are all one.

## Golden Whispers in Dreamland

In the glow of twilight's grace,
Whispers dance in soft embrace.
Stars above begin to gleam,
Cradled in a golden dream.

Gentle breezes softly sway,
Guiding night to greet the day.
Moonlight spills like liquid gold,
Tales of magic, softly told.

Every shadow, every light,
Holds the secrets of the night.
Echos of a distant tune,
Lift the heart beneath the moon.

In this realm where dreams take flight,
Hope ignites the starry night.
Golden whispers, soft and sweet,
Carry lovers' hearts to meet.

As dawn breaks with tender sighs,
Dreamers wake beneath blue skies.
Memories in hearts remain,
Golden whispers call again.

# Enchanted Fields of Dusk

Fields aglow with hues so bright,
Chasing shadows, ending light.
Crickets sing their evening song,
In this world where dreams belong.

Whispers of the night unfold,
Tales of nature, rich and bold.
Flowers sigh in soft embrace,
Lost in time, a sacred space.

The horizon wears a crown,
As the sun sinks gently down.
Waves of lavender and gold,
Hold the secrets yet untold.

Stars appear, a twinkling glow,
Guiding hearts where wild winds blow.
Through enchanted fields we roam,
Finding peace, we make our home.

As the night begins to weave,
Hope and dreams we will believe.
In this dusk, our spirits soar,
Enchanted fields forevermore.

# Serenade of Sunlit Meadows

In meadows lush where flowers play,
The sun ignites the break of day.
Butterflies in colors bright,
Dance and twirl in pure delight.

Gentle streams through grasses flow,
Singing songs we long to know.
Nature's voice, a soothing balm,
Wraps the world in tender calm.

Golden rays upon our skin,
Whispers of the winds begin.
Every petal, every leaf,
Promises of joy and grief.

In this bright and sunlit space,
We find time's divine embrace.
Together, hearts with nature sing,
In this meadow, hope takes wing.

As the day begins to wane,
Peace surrounds us like soft rain.
Serenade of life we share,
Sunlit meadows, purest air.

## Pastel Dreams on Twilight's Edge

On twilight's edge, where colors blend,
Pastel dreams begin to send.
A canvas painted soft and light,
Where shadows play and spirits flight.

Hues of pink and gentle blue,
Whisper secrets deep and true.
In the hush, sweet stories flow,
Of longing hearts and twilight glow.

The horizon kisses night's embrace,
Guarding dreams in fragile space.
As stars emerge, they softly gleam,
Cradling our most cherished dream.

With every breath, the world unwinds,
In pastel scenes, our hope binds.
Finding solace in this hour,
Time stands still within its power.

As night unfolds its velvet cloak,
Pastel dreams in silence cloak.
On twilight's edge, where dreams are spun,
We find our peace, our hearts as one.

www.ingramcontent.com/pod-product-compliance
Ingram Content Group UK Ltd.
Pitfield, Milton Keynes, MK11 3LW, UK
UKHW021323170125
4163UKWH00003B/151

9 781805 594352